3



Story by
**Okura**

Art by
**Coma Hashii**

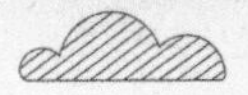

# CONTENTS



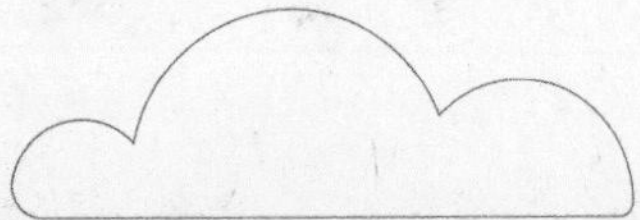

HE IS A HOMO, THOUGH, RIGHT?
RIGHT?
HE TOTALLY HAS TO BE!
HE'S, LIKE, SO GIRLIE!
SO GIRLIE AND CREEPY!
BWAH HA HA HA
Chapter 15: So maybe you mean "weird stuff"?

FWP

RELAX!
THEY'RE NOT TALKING ABOUT YOU.

HUH?

OH, YEAH, I KNOW.
AND I TOTALLY DON'T THINK BEING GAY IS CREEPY!
I KNOW, I KNOW.
Keep your voice down!

You know not all gay guys are, right?
And, like, you're not that girlie, Sanada.
THIS IS KOU SANADA.
HE'S GAY, BUT IT'S A SECRET.
potato & cabbage
restaurant
THE ONLY PEOPLE AT SCHOOL ...
...WHO KNOW ARE ME ...
OH! THEY'RE HERE!
...AND ONE MORE PERSON.
NOSHI-ROOOOO!

MAKOTO MORINAGA, TENTH GRADER, A YEAR BEHIND US.
GEEEEZ! YOU'RE LATE!
WHAT WERE YOU GUYS DOING?!
JUST WALKING OVER LIKE USUAL.
HE'S GAY TOO, AND APPARENTLY, I'M HIS TYPE...

NOSHIRO, SIT BESIDE ME!
S-sure.
HE'S BASICALLY KEEPING THE GAY THING QUIET.
BUT HE'S NOT REALLY TRYING TO HIDE THAT HE LIKES ME.

MORNING, KOU.
HEY.
HER NAME'S AYUMI YAMAMOTO.
SHE'S BEEN GOING TO SCHOOL WITH SANADA SINCE ELEMENTARY.
SHE DOESN'T KNOW THAT HE AND MAKOTO ARE GAY.
Menu

SHE TOLD SANADA SHE LIKES HIM, AND HE TURNED HER DOWN.
EVEN AFTER THAT, THOUGH, THEY'RE STILL CLOSE.
FOR SANADA, SHE'S SOMEONE HE CAN TRUST.
'KAY, SHOULD WE GET STUDYING?
Oh!
HANG ON, NOSHIRO!
MATH II
I MADE SOME QUIZ QUESTIONS SO WE CAN STUDY REALLY SIMPLY.
WE CAN GET DESSERT AND STILL KEEP STUDYING.
KEY POINTS QUIZ GRADE 11
THE RESTAURANT MAYBE WON'T LIKE IT...
...IF WE SPREAD OUT OUR NOTEBOOKS AND STAY FOREVER, SO...
DIG
DIG
I HAVE TENTH GRADE QUESTIONS, TOO.
GRADE 10
WOW!
YAMAMOTO, YOU'RE AMAZING!
TOTALLY!

THAT WAS SCHOOL STUFF, BUT IT WAS SOMEHOW SUPER FUN, HUH?

IT REALLY WAS. I WISH CLASS WAS THAT MUCH FUN.

YOU WANNA GO TO KARAOKE AFTER THIS, NOSHIRO?!

Ohh.

SORRY, I'VE GOT A THING.

SORRY, AYUMI. I MEAN ...

...THAT MUST HAVE BEEN A LOT OF WORK TO MAKE THOSE QUIZ SHEETS JUST FOR US.

UH-UH. I LIKE THAT STUFF.

AND MAKING THE QUESTIONS IS ACTUALLY STUDYING FOR ME.
THAT'S SOMETHING REALLY ...
... AMAZING ABOUT YOU, AYUMI.
I REALLY RESPECT THAT.
THANKS.

MAYBE...

...SINCE YOU MET NOSHIRO ...

...

DUNNO.
I CAN'T TELL WHEN IT'S ME.

OKAY, SEE YOU AT SCHOOL.
GOOD-BYE, NOSHI-ROOOOO!
STATION

WHAT'S THIS THING YOU'VE GOT THEN?
I'M HAVING DINNER WITH HIDE.

WHEN DID YOU TWO GET SO CHUMMY ?!
HE TEXTS ME ALL THE TIME.
AND I'VE GONE TO HIM FOR ADVICE AND STUFF...
HIDE
Noshiro, let's go for dinner again! It's all-you-can-eat!
Sounds good.
I'M GOING, TOO.
ASK HIM IF IT'S OKAY.
Okay...
HIDE IS...
All-you-can-eat shabu-shabu!
SHABU
...A 26-YEAR-OLD OFFICE WORKER...
...AND SANADA'S EX-BOYFRIEND.
HUH, SO YOU GUYS WERE ALL STUDYING TOGETHER?
SOUNDS LIKE YOU'RE TIGHT.
HE'S ALWAYS HELPING ME OUT WHEN I'M STRUGGLING WITH SANADA STUFF OR GAY STUFF.

HUH?!

Ha ha ha

YOU DON'T HAVE TO SHOVEL FOOD DOWN JUST BECAUSE IT'S ALL-YOU-CAN EAT. IT'S OKAY!

OH! YEAH!

CHOMP CHOMP

I'm going to get some veggies!

Noshiro's adorable, huh?

TROT TROT

WHAT? YOU DON'T LIKE ME AND NOSHIRO GETTING CLOSER?
DO YOU ALWAYS WANT THINGS ALL TO YOUR-SELF?

That's not the point!
Hm?
It's not?

IT'S NOT THAT.
I JUST DON'T WANT YOU MESSING AROUND WITH NOSHIRO FOR FUN.
LIKE, TELLING HIM GRAPHIC GAY STUFF.
OR STUFF ABOUT ME...

SO MAYBE YOU MEAN "WEIRD STUFF"?

RELAX.

WE DON'T TALK ABOUT THAT STUFF.

I KNOW IT FEELS SCARY TO HAVE PEOPLE...

...KNOW THINGS YOU DON'T WANT THEM TO KNOW.

BUT IF NOSHIRO WAS INTERESTED IN THAT "WEIRD STUFF"...

...AND HE JUST REALLY HAD TO KNOW?

I GUESS YOU'D AVOID ACTUALLY ANSWERING HIM, HUH, HIKARU?

THIS "WEIRD STUFF" IS AN IMPORTANT PART OF YOU.

YOU MUST ALSO WANT HIM TO KNOW, RIGHT?

I got all kinds of vege-tables!
...
Thanks!

OH, RIGHT.
SO, NOSHIRO?
DO YOU WANT TO GO TO THE SUPER SENTO BATHHOUSE SOMETIME?
MNCH MNCH
?!
GULP

SUPER SENTO!
I'VE NEVER REALLY BEEN. I'D LOVE TO TRY IT!
LET'S GO, SA—
NO!

GRIN
Huh?
HIKARU HATES BATHS AND POOLS AND STUFF LIKE THAT.

HIKARU GETS WEIRDED OUT AROUND GROUPS OF NAKED GUYS.
What?
THAT'S YOU, HIDE!!

AND I TOLD YOU NOT TO TALK ABOUT STUFF LIKE THAT!!
HA HA HA! SOOO-RRY.
SHABU
All-you-can-eat shabu-shabu!

SORRY TO MAKE YOU PAY FOR EVERY-THING!
NO, NO. YOU HAVE TO LET THE GROWN-UP PAY.

THANKS FOR JOINING ME, NOSHIRO.
THANKS FOR INVITING M—
MMPH

WHAT'RE YOU SO AWKWARD ABOUT?

YOU USUALLY LOVE THIS STUFF.

IS THAT WHAT YOU LIKED...

...ABOUT HIDE?

I GUESS.
HMM.
BUT, LIKE, I MAYBE GET THAT...

...

PT

HEY.
WHAT—

SHOVE
HEY! WH— ?!
WHAT ARE YOU DOING ?!

WELP
AAH...
I JUST THOUGHT MAYBE I HAD IT, TOO.
THAT ACCEPTING THING.
HOW ABOUT IT?
HOW WOULD I KNOW?!
DON'T TRY IT OUT ON ME!
HEY, WHY ARE YOU SO MAD?
YOU CAN'T JUST GO HUGGING ME IN FRONT OF PEOPLE!
DON'T GO ACTING LIKE MORI-NAGA!

HIDE DID IT BEFORE, THOUGH.

IS IT OKAY IF IT'S HIDE?

AND, LIKE, WHENEVER I TOUCH YOU...

...YOU ALWAYS ACT LIKE YOU HATE IT.

EE-AAH!!

STOP IT, DUMMY!!

WHUP

THAT HURT! YOU DON'T NEED TO GET SO ANGRY!

I DON'T LIKE BEING TICKLED!

STOP IT! WHAT ARE YOU DOING?!

IS THAT ACTUALLY...

...BECAUSE YOU **LIKE** HIDE...?

I GUESS YOU'D AVOID ACTUALLY ANSWERING HIM, HUH, HIKARU?

NO.
IT'S BECAUSE YOU'RE STRAIGHT.
HUH...?
B-BECAUSE I'M STRAIGHT...
...I CAN'T HUG YOU?
EX-ACTLY.

HUH? WHAT'S THAT ABOUT ...?
I DON'T GET IT.
OF COURSE YOU DON'T.
IF YOU DID GET IT, YOU WOULDN'T DO THAT STUFF.
YOU'RE TOO INNOCENT.
WHEN IT COMES TO GAY STUFF.
WHISPER

WHATEVER THE REASON...
...I DIDN'T WANT TO FORCE SANADA TO DO SOMETHING HE HATED.
I DIDN'T WANT TO.
BUT...

WHEN I SAW HIDE WITH SANADA...

...I CAN'T REALLY PUT IT INTO WORDS... BUT, I DUNNO...

I WAS LIKE, "LUCKY."

LIKE, HIDE'S SPECIAL TO SANADA.

EVEN I GOT THAT SOMEHOW.

HAVE YOU HAD A "SPECIAL FRIEND" BEFORE?

WE'RE HEEEE-EEERE!!

ZIS-NEEEE-EEEY!!

welcome to

Land

## Chapter 16: You wanna do it? With me?

AYUMI... ARE YOU MAYBE ...

TAK TAK

YAMAMOTO, YOU REALLY LOVE ZISNEY, HUH?!

AH!

....!

...

I GUESS IT'S A BIT CHILDISH ...

Zisneyland MAP

OKAY, WE'RE TOTALLY COUNTING ON YOU, YAMAMOTO!

WE'LL FOLLOW YOU TODAY!

PLEASE INSTRUCT US IN THE WAYS OF ZISNEY!

WHP

THIS IS GREAT.
I WAS WORRIED ABOUT TAGGING ALONG...
WHEW
I WOULDN'T HAVE COME IF IT WAS JUST GOING TO BE US THREE GUYS.
HUH?
I'M GLAD YOU CAME, AYUMI.
NOW I DON'T HAVE TO STRESS.
CLUTCH
WHAT'S... THAT MEAN...
W-
OH, I THINK YOU KNOW...
YAY
YAY
THIS PLACE REALLY IS FULL OF COUPLES, HUH?
FWP
FWP
NOSHIRO! I DON'T WANNA BE LEFT OUT. YOU AND ME...!
YANK
HUH?

GRAB

OKAAAY!

LET'S GO!

DON'T SAY STUFF LIKE THAT.

YOU'LL GET MY HOPES UP.

WE'RE GETTING THROUGH THE LINES SO QUICK THANKS TO YAMA-MOTO.
AS LONG AS I'M WITH YOU, NOSHIRO, I'M COOL WITH STANDING IN LINE, TOO!

NOOOO.
COME ON. DON'T BE LIKE THAT.

NO WAY, DUMMY.
BUT YOU LIKE ME! COME ON!
NO ONE'S WATCH-ING.
HON-ESTLY.

AAAH, LOOK! PEOPLE ARE WATCHING!
DON'T WORRY. IT DOESN'T MATTER.
?!!

...
N—
NOSHIRO!
WE CAN'T LET THEM BEAT US...!
?!

WHUK
...
That hurt, Sanada!

WHEE
AAAAH
SPLOOSH

EEEEE! SO CUTE!

I'VE BEEN DYING TO EAT THIS FOR AAAAGES!
IT'S CUTE, BUT ISN'T IT KINDA EXPENSIVE?
...
WHAT'S WRONG, NOSHIRO?

YOU'VE BEEN PRETTY QUIET.
HUH?!
I HAVE? IT'S NOTHING...
HA HA HA...?

ARE YOU MAYBE NOT OKAY WITH THE SCARY RIDES, NOSHIRO?
MNCH MNCH
WHAT? I'M SORRY!
IF YOU'D TOLD ME, WE COULD HAVE DONE DIFFERENT THINGS...
NO, NO! IT'S NOT THAT!

IT'S NOT THAT...
AH...
NAH, UH...

YOU'RE SO CUTE!!
YOU'RE, LIKE, SO PURE!!
You're gonna give me a nose-bleed!!
KLATTER
Shut up.
I— IT WAS A SURPRISE TO HAVE THEM DO IT RIGHT IN FRONT OF US, THOUGH.
AH
H-HAVE YOU...
NO WAY... YOU ALL—!
SEEING THAT KISS CLOSE-UP...
I WAS JUST THINKING... THAT'S MAYBE THE FIRST TIME I...

YOU'VE ALL KISSED SOMEONE ?!
WELL ...
I WAS GOING OUT WITH SOME-ONE.
WHAT ?
AH
CRAP...
I'VE KISSED SOME-ONE, TOO!
THE FIRST TIME WAS WITH THIS GIRL IN THE NEIGH-BORHOOD, THOUGH.
I...
APPAR-ENTLY, I ALWAYS USED TO KISS MY DAD WHEN I WAS LITTLE.
KOFF
SEE?
IT'S REALLY NOT SO WEIRD AS ALL THAT.

NOSHIRO, YOU STILL HAVEN'T ?!
MMM.
OKAY, THEN. I'LL BE...
...YOUR FIRST...
KRK

...?
WHAT?
!
OH! UM!
NOSHI-ROOOOO!
GAH
AGH HRN

THIS IS AMAZ-ING! C'MERE! OVER HERE!
HUH?
WHAT? WHAT?!

TAK TAK

K—

KOU.
YOU WERE GOING OUT WITH SOME-ONE...?

...
HOW ...?
OH... UM... UH...
Oh! Wow!
So it's like art on the water, huh?
I'VE NEVER SEEN YOU WITH SOMEONE.
I WAS KINDA SURPRISED ...

UH...
...I DO HAVE A LIFE AND STUFF.
WHY...
...DIDN'T I THINK ABOUT THAT?

WITH WHO?

SOMEONE FROM CLASS?

SOMEONE I KNOW?

ARE THEY STILL TOGETHER?

I'M DONE.

I JUST CAN'T.

I'M FEELING REGRET ALL OVER AGAIN!

MAYBE IT'S THE MAGIC OF ZISNEY.

WHAT DOES A KISS ...

...FEEL LIKE?

I MEAN, I LIKE MAKOTO.
BUT A KISS IS MORE... UM...
THAT'S SOMETHING YOU DO WITH SOMEONE SPECIAL!
Heh
IF THAT'S WHAT YOU'RE THINKING ...
...YOU CAN JUST CHECK WHAT IT FEELS LIKE...
...WITH THE PERSON YOU WANT TO DO IT WITH...
...AT THE TIME WHEN YOU WANT TO DO IT.

AAAAH.
I GUESS YOU'RE RIGHT, BUT, LIKE...
I FEEL KINDA LIKE...
...I'M SUPER LATE TO THE PARTY...
SIIIGH
HUH. SO YOU'RE AWARE OF IT AT LEAST.
AAH. SEE? I KNEW IT.
I THOUGHT YOU WEREN'T INTER-ESTED IN STUFF LIKE THAT.
I AM IN MY OWN WAY, OKAY?
HMM...
SO THEN...

YOU WANNA DO IT?
WITH ME?

WHA-
WHAT ARE YOU-
SHF
HUH ?!
YANK
UH, HEY-

YANK

I'M KIDDING.
PiYo!!
PiYo!

D—
DON'T TEASE ME! SERIOUS-LYYYYY!
Aaaaaah.
I WAS KIDDING, BUT...

...THAT'S WHAT BEING GAY IS LIKE.

...

We got so much stuff!
Sorry to take so long!

KATUNK
KATUNK

KATUNK
KATUNK

KATUNK
KATUNK

YOU WANNA DO IT?
WITH ME?
I MEAN, A KISS.
IS IT REALLY SOMETHING YOU CAN JUST "DO" LIKE THAT?

SANADA'S GOT LOTS OF EXPE-RIENCE, THOUGH.
SO MAYBE IT'S NO BIG DEAL FOR HIM.

BUT...
...I WONDER IF HE'D WANNA DO IT WITH SOMEONE HE DOESN'T LIKE?
WOULD HE EVEN SUGGEST THAT TO SOMEONE HE DOESN'T LIKE?
DOES HE "LIKE" ME...
...MAYBE JUST A LITTLE?
Ah
Zisney land

I'M KIDDING.
A COUNTRY POTATO LIKE YOU IS TOTALLY NOT MY TYPE.
BUT.
HE DID SAY THAT, SO...
FWUMP
WELL, WHATEVER.
I DON'T GET IT!
SNR SNR
KATUNK
KATUNK
ARE THEY REALLY JUST FRIENDS, THOUGH?
VERY SUSPICIOUS!

WH—

WHAT WAS THAT...?

WHY...

MAYBE THAT RUMOR THAT HE'S A HOMO IS TRUE?!

WHY DIDN'T I...

...THINK OF THAT?

RUGBY PLAYERS'RE HOT!
Chapter 17: It's Kou.
I MEAN, LIKE, HATAKE-MURA'S ALWAYS ON TV, SO YOU KNOW HIM, YEAH?
BLAH
I'M A FAN OF TAKANO, THOUGH!
Oh! I LIKE KAWAJI, TOO!
BLAH
BUT MY FAVE'S GOTTA BE...
BLAH
BLAH
WHAM
YAMANAKA
HIS POWERFUL PRESENCE
...YAMANAKA THE JUDO STAR!
SO COOL!
...
SPORTS CLUB

A ROUND FACE WITH PERFECT LINES!

THE SIMPLE YET ELEGANT...

...EYES...

...NOSE...

...AND THIN LIPS!

AND...

...A FAT BODY THAT MAKES ITS PRESENCE KNOWN! IT'S BIG AND MUSCLY!

YOU'RE THE BEST, NOSHIRO!!

GAAAAAH

AAAH

HIDE
I SAW A PICTURE OF YOUR EX.
AND I THOUGHT HE WAS COOL, TOO!
YOU AND I ARE MAYBE INTO THE SAME TYPE, YEAAAAAH?
IN WHICH CASE, WHEN IT COMES TO NOSHIRO...
...YOU SHOULD BE—
BUT, SANADA...
...YOU LIKE GUYS WITH BIG BODIES, TOO, RIGHT?
NOSHIRO.
SORRY.
COULD I HAVE SOME MORE TEA?
OH... S-SURE.

SLAM
MORI-NAGA.
...
WHAT ARE YOU UP TO?!
WHAT DO YOU MEAA-AAAN?
I WAS JUST THINKING MAYBE YOU WERE INTO HIM. YOU KNOOOOW.
I...
...DON'T FALL FOR STRAIGHT GUYS.

CAN YOU ACTUALLY THINK YOU WON'T LIKE SOMEONE...

...AND THEN JUST NOT LIKE THEM?

OKAY, THEN. IF NOSHIRO WAS GAY...
...WOULD YOU LIKE HIM?

ISN'T IT TOO SOON...
...TO JUST GIVE UP OR WHATEVS?
BUT IF THAT'S YOUR RULE, SANADA...
...THEN I GUESS I DON'T HAVE TO WORRY ABOUT YOU, HUH?
KA-CHAK
I'M BACK.
AND I BROUGHT SNACKS!

Yay! Snacks!

...

HMM...
MANLY MEN ARE PRETTY COOL, HUH...

"YOU'RE THE BEST, NOSHIRO !!"
"YOU AND I ARE MAYBE INTO THE SAME TYPE, YEAAAAAH ?"
SQUOOSH
...
UM...
LIE ON YOUR STOMACH.
AND LIFT YOUR UPPER BODY...
SPECIAL!
The talk of the town!
Effective workouts you can do at home
Start today!
HNGH !
YANK!

I'VE NEVER WORRIED ...

...ABOUT MY LOOKS BEFORE.

YOU'RE TOTALLY NOT MY TYPE.

BUT.

I CAN'T JUST LEAVE IT LIKE THAT.

IT'S BUGGING ME FOR SOME REASON!

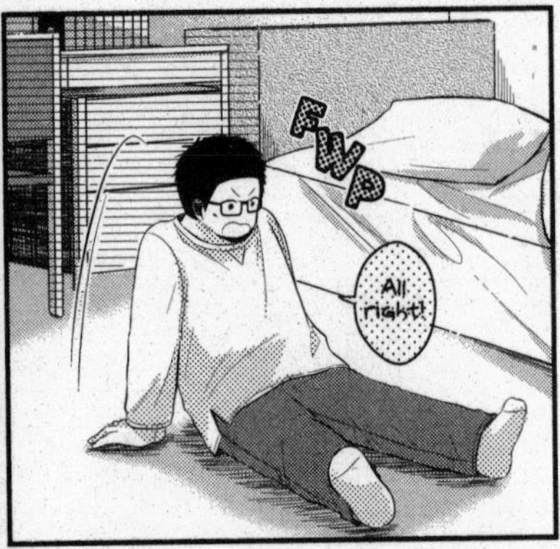

WHAT?! YOU WENT TO ZISNEY ?!
WITH SANADA ?!
IT WASN'T JUST US.
NOSHIRO AND MORINAGA CAME, TOO.
OHHH.
BUT YOU WERE THE ONLY GIRL, AYUMI? WEIRD GROUP.
THOK
NO, THE FOUR OF THEM HAVE A STUDY GROUP.
THEY'RE PRETTY CLOSE, Y'KNOW ?
THOK
CLOSE...
IS THAT ALL?
THAT ...
DID I JUST SEE IT WRONG ?

IT LOOKED LIKE NOSHIRO...
...WAS ABOUT TO KISS KOU.
SO NOSHIRO HAS FEELINGS...
...OF MORE THAN FRIENDSHIP FOR KOU ?!
WHEN I THINK ABOUT IT, I WAS JUST TOTALLY WORRYING ABOUT KOU...
WHAT WAS SANADA LIKE IN JUNIOR HIGH?
...AND I WAS GLAD NOSHIRO WANTED TO GET TO KNOW HIM.
THE TWO OF THEM GOT CLOSER, AND I...
IT JUST MAKES SENSE THAT I WAS FEELING PANICKED!

......
NOO... THAT'S TOTALLY NOT IT.
WHAT ARE YOU GUYS TALKING ABOUT?
WHAT GIRLS HE LIKES.
WHA—?!
I'LL WATCH FOR THE RIGHT TIME TO TAKE OFF. THEN YOU AND SANADA GO AROUND THE FESTIVAL ON YOUR OWN. JUST THE TWO OF YOU.
GOOD LUCK!
O-OKAY. THANKS!
NOSHIRO'S NOT LIKE THAT.
I EVEN SAID IT WAS RIDICULOUS. THERE'S NO WAY.
AND THAT RUMOR ABOUT KOU, TOO.
I'M SURE IT'S JUST A MISUNDER-STANDING...
I HAD TO LAUGH AT THE WHOLE THING.
HEY?
AYUMI, DO YOU STILL LIKE SANADA?
ALL KINDS OF LOOSE ENDS THERE!
HEY, BUT, LIKE...
WHAT?!
BA-DMP

SANADA ...
...DOESN'T SEEM INTERESTED IN GIRLS, THOUGH.
OH, THAT'S TRUE.
TO THE POINT WHERE THERE'S THAT RUMOR HE'S GAY.
IT'S LIKE HE GETS IT OR SOME-THING.
COM-PARED WITH THE DUMB BOYS OVER THERE...
...HE SEEMS MORE GROWN-UP.
Oh yeah! Totally!
"SANADA DOESN'T SEEM INTERESTED IN GIRLS."
RIGHT.
THAT'S KOU.

HE HAD A GIRLFRIEND.

WITHOUT ME KNOWING...

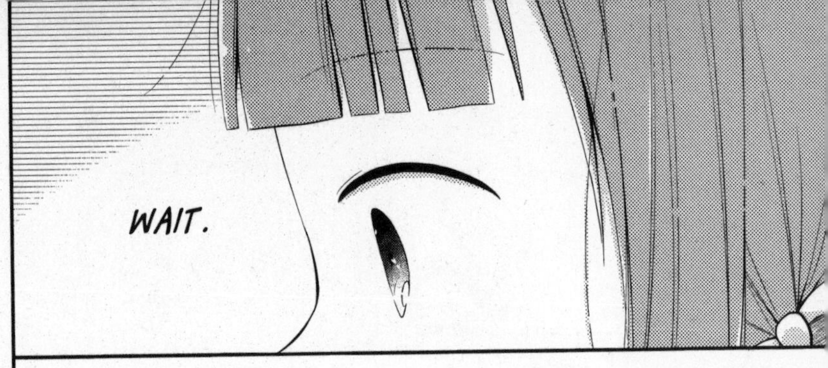

GIRLFRIEND?

DID KOU...

...SAY "GIRLFRIEND"?

OH!

YAMA-MOTOOO-OO!

SUP! WHAT'S GOING ON?

MORINAGA. UM...

YOU MIND IF I ASK YOU SOMETHING?

TROT TROT

BEFORE, YOU...

YOU ASKED IF...

...KOU AND NOSHIRO WERE JUST FRIENDS.

SO I WAS JUST WONDERING.

WHAT...

...DID YOU THINK WAS "SUSPICIOUS"?

DASH

THAT'S TOTALLY IT.

NOTHING GOING ON WITH THOSE TWO.

SANADA'S GONNA DRAG HIS FEET...

...SO I'M GONNA SNATCH UP NOSHIRO!

SANADA DOESN'T SEEM INTERESTED IN GIRLS.
...
KOU...
THUMP
...NEVER TALKED TO ME ABOUT THAT STUFF...
...SO SOMEWHERE IN MY HEART, I WAS RELIEVED.
SO I...
THUMP
...NEVER THOUGHT ABOUT IT.
THUMP
UH...
...I DO HAVE A LIFE AND STUFF.

YOU'RE NOT ON MY RADAR LIKE THAT.
I'M...
...NOT THE GUY YOU THINK I AM.
I MADE SURE...
...NOT TO THINK ABOUT IT.

IT'S NOT NOSHIRO.
IT'S KOU.
I WANT TO KNOW EVERYTHING ABOUT KOU.
NO.
I DON'T WANT TO KNOW.
I WANT TO KNOW, AND YET...

CHATTER
UGH. ART FESTIVAL. BOOORING.
CHATTER
CHATTER
I JUST WANNA GO HOME.
SKY BLUE ART THEATER
Chapter 18: Yeah.
Music of Star

AAAH, I ALMOST FELL ASLEEP!
TRUDGE
DID YOU UNDER-STAND ANY OF THAT?
SHE WAS SEXY!
TRUDGE
THE LAST BIT WAS JUST, **OKAY**, WE GET IT.

CHATTER
CHATTER
SANADA! SANADA!

THE ACTOR WITH THE BEARD PLAYING THE DAD.
HE'S TOTALLY YOUR TYPE, RIGHT?!

...!
WHAT ?!

HUH? HE'S NOT?
HIDE SAID YOU LIKED GUYS WITH BEARDS.
WELL...
I DIDN'T SAY YOU WERE WRONG.
WHY ARE YOU SUD-DENLY—
OH! HEY! LOOK!
MR. TERA-YAMA, RIGHT?
THAT GYM TEACHER'S HERE!
SO WHAT IF HE IS?
WHAT?
THAT TEACHER'S YOUR TYPE, YEAH?
OH!
WHAT ABOUT THAT GUY?!
HE'S SUPER SOLID.
MAYBE HE'S YOUR TYPE, TOO?!

SHUT UP.
SO WHAT IF ANY OF THEM ARE MY TYPE?
YOU THINK I JUST GET ALL HORNY OVER ANY GUY SO LONG AS HE'S MY TYPE?
YOU DON'T GET TO HAVE FUN WITH THIS.
...!
WHA- ?!

THAT LOOK ON YOUR FACE LIKE YOU THINK YOU KNOW SOMETHING ...

IT'S TOTALLY ANNOYING.

WH–

HUH ?!

WHY DO YOU CARE WHAT MY TYPE IS?

...!

IT'S...

...JUST ...

I MEAN ...

ONCE YOU'VE FINISHED YOUR ART FESTIVAL REPORTS, YOU CAN GO HOME.
OKAY.
HMPH
HMM
WHAT IS GOING ON WITH YOU TWO?
YOU'RE POUTING LIKE YOU'RE FIVE OR SOMETHING...
Come on
I'M GOING TO THE WASHROOM!
S-SURE.
NOSHI-ROOOOO!

HELLO, NOSHIRO!
Hi!
HUH?
WHERE'S SANADA? YOU'RE NOT TOGETHER?
WHP WHP

NO IDEA.
WHAT-EVER. WHO CARES ABOUT HIM?!
HUH?!

AH!

RIGHT!
LET'S JUST LEAVE SANADA BE!

CAN I COME OVER AGAIN, NOSHIRO?!

OF COURSE! FINALS ARE OVER AND ALL!

Let's hang out!

2-2

HUH?

KOU.

...
WHERE ARE NOSHIRO AND MORI-NAGA?
NO IDEA.

SOME-THING HAPPEN?
WITH NOSHIRO ?

NOTHING.

WHO EVEN CARES ABOUT THAT GUY ANYWAY?

Hee hee.

WHAT?

OH, SORRY.

IT'S JUST...

YOU ACTUALLY CARE ABOUT NOSHIRO, HUH?

HUH ...?

IT'S LIKE, YOU DON'T EVER ...
...GET TOO HUNG UP ON ANYONE, KOU.
I'VE NEVER ACTUALLY SEEN YOU...
...GET MAD AT SOMEONE.

IT'S ONLY WITH NOSHIRO ...
NOSHIRO WAS ALL UPSET.
IT'S HIS FAULT.
...THAT YOU GET WORKED UP LIKE THIS.

I GUESS...
...NOSHIRO'S PRETTY SPECIAL TO YOU?

FSSSH
... WH—
WHAT'S THAT ... ... SUPPOSED TO MEAN ?
MM-MM. NOTHING.
TAK
LET'S GO.

AYU—
KOU.
KOU.

DO YOU LIKE BOYS?

YEAH.

I WANTED TO...
...ACTUALLY TELL YOU MYSELF, AYUMI...

PLIP
PLIP

ME, TOO.
I WAS SCARED TO ASK.
I DIDN'T WANT TO KNOW.
BUT IT WAS DRIVING ME NUTS!
BUT NOW...
...THAT YOU'RE SAYING IT'S TRUE...
...I FEEL RELIEVED THAT WHAT I WAS FEELING...
...WAS RIGHT!
AAAH, HONESTLY.
I'M SO PATHETIC.
Ha ha ha

OKAY.
SO NOSHIRO KNOWS, TOO.
SORRY.
IT WAS HARDER TO TELL YOU BECAUSE WE'VE KNOWN EACH OTHER FOR SO LONG...
NO, EVERYTHING MAKES SENSE NOW.

NOT BECAUSE ...
...YOU LIKE HIM?

I MIGHT IF IT WAS MORI-NAGA.
I DON'T WANT TO IMAGINE THAT.
Come on...

AND EVEN IF...
...I DID HATE IT...

...AND YOU SAID, "WELL, DOESN'T THAT MEAN YOU WANT TO GO OUT WITH HIM"...
...I CAN'T IMAGINE THAT, EITHER.

TO BEGIN WITH, IT'S NOT EVEN A POSSI-BILITY.
NOSHIRO'S STRAIGHT. HE DOESN'T SEE ME LIKE THAT.

MAYBE.
YOU CAN'T KNOW THAT, THOUGH.
...
I DON'T WANT NOSHIRO TO BE GAY OR ANYTHING.
I THINK IT'D BE TOTALLY GREAT IF HE STARTED GOING OUT WITH SOME GIRL.
IT'S OKAY...
...AS LONG AS WE CAN STAY THE WAY WE ARE NOW.

THE WAY...
...WE ARE NOW...
MAYBE IT'S THE SAME FOR ME.
WITH YOU.

LIKE THIS.

NO.

KOU.

I...

SO, LIKE...
...WHEN I HEARD YOU'D BEEN GOING OUT WITH SOMEONE...
...I WAS RELIEVED WHEN I FOUND OUT...
...IT WAS A GUY.

IF IT HAD BEEN A GIRL...
...THEN I'D HATE IT. LIKE, WHY NOT ME THEN?

IF YOU ONLY FALL FOR...
...BOYS, KOU...

...THEN MAYBE I CAN BE...
...YOUR NUMBER ONE GIRL.

WH—
WHAT AM I EVEN TALKING ABOUT?!
SHF SHF
S-SORRY! JUST FORGET IT!
AYUMI!

THAT MAKES ME SUPER HAPPY.

THANKS.

BUT.

I CAN'T SAY SOMETHING SO IRRESPONSIBLE...

SORRY.

I DON'T KNOW...

...IF I CAN SAY YOU'RE NUMBER ONE.

BUT YOU'RE THE ONLY GIRL...

...WHO KNOWS I'M GAY.

UH-HUH.
I WON'T TELL ANYONE.

BZZ
BZZ

NOSHIRO
Makoto's coming over to my place tomorrow.
17:37
What about you?!
17:37

SIGH
WHAT?

TAP
TAP
BUT IT'S FINE...
...THE WAY IT IS.
17:37
17:37
I'll come.
17:39
SO WHY DO YOU...
...MAKE ME HAPPY LIKE THIS?

I MEAN, MAKING A FACE LIKE THAT...
...WHEN HE'S JUST TOLD ME...
...THERE'S ZERO CHANCE.
SO CUTE...
SQUEEZE
HE LET HIS GUARD DOWN.
AND HE GETS TO BE ALL FREE.
IT'S NOT FAIR.

AAH.
IT'S...
...HOPELESS, HUH...
AAAH.
THIS SUCKS.
STUPID KOU.

## Chapter 19: A classmate's better.

18:43
85%
MAKOTO
I'm so sad that I don't get to see you over winter break!
I want to sleep over at your place!
SEND

Family Resta

WOW!
THIS KID'S PRETTY PROACTIVE, HUH?

PROACTIVE?
YEAH.
I MEAN, HE LIKES YOU, RIGHT?

AND THE FACT THAT HE WANTS TO SLEEP OVER, THAT MEANS—
Hey!
HIDE! I TOLD YOU TO QUIT THAT!
?

SO? WHAT'RE YOU GOING TO DO?
YOU ANSWER HIM?

NOT YET. COULD BE FUN, THOUGH.
DUNNO.

IF WE STAY UP TOO LATE, MY PARENTS'LL COMPLAIN ABOUT THE NOISE.
MY SISTER ACTUALLY JUST TOLD ME...
YOUR FRIENDS ARE SO NOISY.
SO THERE'S THAT...
Me and you make...
...the best team!
He is incapable of being quiet.

I'M TELLING YOU NOW.
I WON'T COME.
CHMP
CHMP
WHAT?! WHY NOT?!
I'D FEEL BAD FOR GETTING IN THE WAY OF YOUR QUALITY TIME WITH MORINAGA.

WHAA-AAT?! THE MORE THE MERRIER, THOUGH!
TOO MANY PEOPLE IN YOUR ROOM IS ANNOY-ING!
SO THEN HOW ABOUT YOU ALL STAY OVER AT MY PLACE?

WHAT ?!
THE MORE THE MERRIER, RIGHT?
GRIN

AAAAAH.

GLOOOOOM

I'M SO EXCITED FOR A SLEEPOVER!

KA-CHAK
COME ON IN!

...!
Hello!

YOU MUST BE THE FAMOUS MAKOTO.
NICE TO MEET YOU. I'M HIDE.
N-NICE TO MEET YOU!

I'M JUST GOING TO RUN OUT AND PICK UP SOME STUFF FOR DINNER. KEEP AN EYE ON THINGS, HIKARU.
HELP YOUR-SELVES TO WHAT-EVER'S IN THE FRIDGE.
GOT IT.

SLAM
...
TH-THAT'S YOUR EX...
Aaaah
HE'S BIGGER THAN I THOUGHT ...
YOU FALLING FOR HIM?
WH—
WHAT ARE YOU TALKING ABOUT ?!
I'M NOT THAT FICKLE!
CHAK

DID YOU USED TO STAY OVER A LOT, SANADA?
PTAN
WELL...

Aah.
SO YOU HAD SOME GOOD TIMES, HUH?
Nice.
OHH...
I'M NOT TALKING ABOUT THAT.
HUNH, MAYBE... NOW THAT HE MENTIONS IT...

I'M BACK!

RSTLE RSTLE
SORRY IT TOOK SO LONG.
I'LL GET TO WORK ON SUPPER.

HIDE CAN COOK, HUH!
YEAH, HE LIKES IT.

Whoa. Amazing.

CHK
CHK
CHK
DAWOON

SIZZZ
BRBLE
BRBLE
OH, HIKARU?
COULD YOU GET SOME PLATES OUT?

CAN I DO ANYTHING TO HELP?!
NO, THAT'S OKAY. THANKS.

GET THE DEEP ONES.
WHICH?
THE ONES WITH THE PATTERN.

THUMP

HUH...

WHY...

SANADA, WERE YOU EATING GREAT FOOD LIKE THIS EVERY DAY?!
I'm super jealous!
NOT EVERY DAY. DUH.
WELL, TODAY I WENT A LITTLE OVER THE TOP.

Hikaru likes omurice, though!
Would you shut up?!

MNCH

YOU WANT SOME MORE, NOSHIRO?
OH! YES, PLEASE!

SCARF SCARF SCARF SCARF

OHH.
THE REASON HIKARU HAD THAT GAY MAGAZINE.

HE BORROWED IT WHEN HE STAYED OVER ONE NIGHT.
AND HE JUST WENT TO SCHOOL WITH IT LIKE THAT.
WOW.
YOU'RE USUALLY SO CAUTIOUS, SANADA.
PRETTY CARE-LESS TO DO THAT, HUH?

CAU-TIOUS?
GRIN
OH, IS THAT THE CHARACTER YOU'RE PLAYING NOW?
IT'S NOT A CHARACTER!!

CHOMP CHOMP
WHAAAT? YOU WERE SO CUTE AND FULL OF SMILES WHEN WE MET, THOUGH!
AND I KEEP TELLING YOU THAT WAS FORCED!

I THINK I HAVE SOME PICS FROM BACK THEN.
YOU WANNA SEE?
KLATTER
I DO! I DO! I DO!!
BAM
QUIT IT! FOR REAL!!

STOP MESSING AROUND, DUMMY!!
WHAA-AAT?
JUST A LITTLE PEEK WON'T HUUUURT!
THUMP
WHY...?
SOME-THING'S OFF...
...WITH ME AGAIN.

SO THEN, HIKARU?

DO YOU WANT TO GET IN WITH ME?

LIKE BEFORE.

WH—
WHAT ARE YOU TALKING ABOUT, HIDE—
I-I...!
I ATE TOO MUCH.
I'M GONNA GO RUN OUTSIDE.
BAMM
HUH?
H-HEY, NOSHIRO?
N-NOSHIRO?!
DASH

HIKARU, WOULD YOU GO WITH NOSHIRO?

AND BRING HIM A COAT OR SOMETHING.

Here Money.

...?

OKAY...

SLAM

HUH?

UM!

NERVOUS

NERVOUS

UH...?

YOU GONNA GET IN THE BATH?
HUUUH?!
BA-DMP

I-I CAN'T!
I MEAN, I'M, TOTALLY DEVOTED TO NOSHIRO!
Please don't distract me!
NO, I DIDN'T MEAN TO-GETHER.
Ha ha ha!

S-i-i-i-i-gh

!
WHUMP

WHAT'S UP WITH YOU ALL OF A SUDDEN?

YOU'RE RIGHT.

WHAT IS GOING ON WITH ME?

I DON'T REALLY GET IT MYSELF.

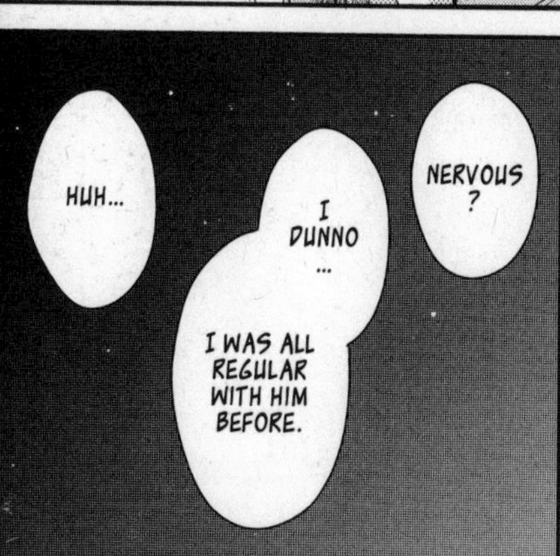

I...
MAYBE I'M JUST NOT GOOD WITH HIDE.

SO LIKE...
IT HASN'T REALLY CLICKED FOR ME BEFORE.
BUT TODAY, I FEEL LIKE I KINDA GET IT.
YOU AND HIDE...
YOU REALLY WERE GOING OUT, HUH?
DID YOU REALLY TAKE BATHS TOGETHER AND STUFF?
...

OKAY, MAYBE THERE WERE TIMES LIKE THAT!
C'mon!
...
SO, SANADA?
DO YOU STILL LIKE HIDE?

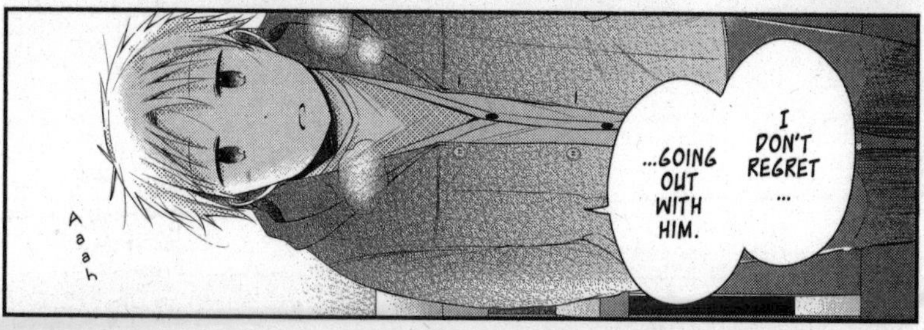


BUT A CLASSMATE'S BETTER FOR DATING.

I—
I MEAN, CLASS-MATES LIKE...

ALL KINDS OF THINGS GO BETTER WHEN YOU'RE CLOSER IN AGE!
WHIRL
AH!
SANADA!

HAVE YOU EVER GONE OUT WITH A CLASS-MATE?

OF COURSE NOT.

YOU'RE THE FIRST PERSON...

...I CAME OUT TO, AFTER ALL.

Oh!
YOU'RE BACK!

NOSHIRO, THAT TOOK FOR-EVEEER!

I ALREADY HAD MY BAAA-AATH!

Oh!
RIGHT. HEY, GUYS?

And I wanted to take it with you!

Sorry ...

I'm gonna jump in, too.

I ONLY HAVE TWO FUTONS.

SO DOES SOMEONE WANT TO SHARE MY BED?

DOUBLE BED

OR ELSE TWO OF YOU'LL HAVE TO SLEEP ON ONE FUTON.

WHAT DO YOU WANT TO DO?

You're really cute.

I- I can't!

Mwah ha ha ha ha!

Noshi-roooo!

# Chapter 20: That's great.

NO WAY!
THIS WHOLE TIME, I THOUGHT THE FUTURE PART MEANT IT WAS NOT ACTUALLY GOOD FORTUNE.
Gaaaah
Pft
SERIOUSLY?
HA HA HA

THAT'S WHY I END UP THINKING IT'S A GOOD DAY WHEN...

...SANADA, THE BOY WHO DOESN'T LAUGH, ACTUALLY LAUGHS.

AAAH! IT'S SO NICE OUT TODAY!

NOSHIIIIII!

ROOOOO!!

LUNGE

Whoa!

See ya!

YEAH. YOU'RE ALWAYS HANGING OUT TOGETHER.
GIVE NACCHI THE CHANCE TO TALK TO HIM SOME-TIMES, TOO.
?
?
WHAT...? WHY...?

COME OOOOON!

YOU'RE NO FAIR, MORIRIN!
HUH?

HUH? MORIRIN.
YOU HAVE TO HAVE NOTICED.
EVER SINCE THE SCHOOL FESTIVAL...
...NACCHI'S BEEN INTO NOSHIRO...

IT'S NOT LIKE HE BELONGS TO YOU.
YOU DON'T GET TO MONOPOLIZE HIM.

2-5

CHATTER CHATTER

See you tomorrow!

Bye!

ONLY THREE MORE MONTHS OF THIS CLASS, HUH?

I'M EXCITED FOR THE CLASS CHANGE, BUT SAD, TOO.

YOU'RE SO OPTIMISTIC.

IT'S GONNA GET ROUGH, WITH ENTRANCE EXAMS AND ALL.

Y-YEAH, BUT FORGET THAT FOR NOW...

IT'D BE GREAT IF WE WERE IN THE SAME CLASS AGAIN, HUH?

Heh.

YEAH.

I GOTTA KEEP AN EYE ON YOU AND MORINAGA.

I DON'T KNOW WHAT YOU'LL GET UP TO, OTHERWISE.

WHAT? ME, TOO?

TOUTOR
COFFEE SHOP

VWWWN

Please seat yourself!

SORRY TO MAKE YOU WAIT TILL PRACTICE WAS OVER.

IT'S TOTALLY FINE.

A GIRL IN MY CLASS ...
...LIKES NOSHIRO, I GUESS.
SHE ASKED ME TO HELP HER...
...GET TO KNOW HIM.

SO?
...
WHAT DO YOU MEAN, SO?
YOU'RE OKAY WITH THIS?

NOSHIRO'S SO NICE.
HE'LL BE FRIENDLY WITH HER.
GUESS SO.
AND SHE'LL ASK HIM OUT.
PROB'LY.
THEY MIGHT START GOING OUT, THOUGH!
MAYBE.
...!
CLENCH
THAT WOULDN'T ...
...BOTHER YOU AT ALL?!

...
YEAH.
I'D PROBABLY BE RELIEVED.

IS THAT BECAUSE ...
...THEN YOU COULD GIVE UP ON NOSHIRO ?
MMMMPH
WELL, I HATE IT!
I MEAN, THE GUY I LIKE GOING OUT WITH SOMEONE ELSE!
THEN JUST DON'T HELP HER GET TO KNOW HIM.
WHY ARE YOU TALKING TO ME ABOUT THIS?

BECAUSE I WANTED YOU TO SAY YOU HATE IT!
I MEAN, I CAN SAY IT.
AND I'M...
...NO ONE TO NOSHIRO!

I DON'T WANT TO GET IN THE WAY OF ANYONE'S TRUE LOVE.
I'M NOT IN A POSITION TO GET IN THE WAY, EITHER!
IT'S ...
...THE SAME FOR ME.
WHOEVER NOSHIRO ENDS UP LIKING...
...WHOEVER HE GOES OUT WITH...
...THAT'S FOR NOSHIRO TO DECIDE.

CHATTER
CHATTER

I'M NOT...

...GIVING UP.

I NEVER HAD HOPE...

...TO BEGIN WITH.

HUFF
HUFF

HUFF
HUFF
HUFF

DING
DONG

KA CHAK
MAKOTO ?!

WHY ARE YOU HERE?
OHHH.

Heh heh heh
I JUST WANTED TO SEE YOU!

HUH.
IT'S JUST FUTURE GOOD FORTUNE, NOT FAKE.
OF COURSE.
WHY DID I JUST FIND THAT OUT NOW?

NO. THEY HAVE TO BE OUT THERE!
DELAYED FORTUNES!
Hngh

SQUEEZE
NOSHIRO.
I LIKE YOU.

UH-
HUH.
THANKS.
AM
I...
...NO
GOOD
?
HUH
...?
I
WANT
YOU...
...ALL TO
MYSELF,
NOSHIRO!
I WANT
YOU TO
GO OUT
WITH
ME!

I...
I LIKE YOU, MAKOTO.
AND IT MAKES ME HAPPY TO HEAR THAT YOU LIKE ME.

BUT...

SHF

HEH HEH HEH.

I KNOW.

YOU MAKE...
...EVERY DAY FUN.

Heh heh heh!

THAT'S ...

...GREAT THEN!

YAH
YAH
YAH

KLATTER

WHERE'D YOU GO?

Okay.
LET'S GO ALREADY.

NOSHIRO?
S—
THIS GIRL...
...FROM MAKOTO'S CLASS...
...TOLD ME SHE LIKES ME.

SO WE'RE GOING OUT NOW...
...I GUESS.

THAT'S GOOD THOUGH, RIGHT?

A GIRL'S NEVER TOLD YOU SHE LIKES YOU BEFORE.

YOU MUST'VE BEEN HAPPY, YEAH?

THAT'S GREAT.

SANADA WAS SMILING.
BUT I FELT KINDA UPSET SOMEHOW.
MAYBE JUST BECAUSE IT WAS CLOUDY THAT DAY.

I NEVER REALLY THOUGHT ...
...THIS DAY WOULD COME.
STATION
THAT I...
...WOULD ...
...HAVE A G-GIRL-FRIEND.
NOSHI-ROOOOO!
Chapter 21: I want to touch you.
SHE'S IN TENTH GRADE, IN MAKOTO'S CLASS.
NATSU AIKAWA.

SHE SUDDENLY CAME ...
...AND TOLD ME SHE LIKED ME...
UM!
EVER SINCE YOU...
...HELPED US AT THE SCHOOL FESTIVAL ...

...I HAVEN'T STOPPED THINKING ABOUT YOU!

Oh!
IT WASN'T ME WHO BROUGHT MAKOTO BACK, THOUGH.
BUT YOU SPENT ALL THAT TIME RUNNING AROUND TOO, RIGHT?!
IT MADE ME REALIZE YOU'RE REALLY NICE.

UM!
SO, UH...
BASI-CALLY... UM!
I—!
I LIKE YOU, NOSHIRO!
WHAAAT?!

I DUNNO. IT'S JUST...
THAT SURPRISED ME.
UM! SO THEN...!
IS THAT A PROB-LEM?!
N-NO! NOT AT ALL!
TH-THANKS...
IF YOU... DON'T HATE THE IDEA...
...WILL YOU PLEASE GO OUT WITH ME?!
?!!

AH! YOU DO HATE IT!!
Waaa aaah
NO! UH!
I DON'T HATE IT!

I DON'T HATE IT...

R—
REALLY?!

FWP
KSH
KSH
?!
I DID IIIIIIIT!
WAAAAAH
CONGRATS, NACCHI!
I NEVER THOUGHT YOU'D ACTUALLY TELL HIM!
...

IT'S LIKE, I JUST COULDN'T STOP!
I'M SO GLAD YOU GOT UP THE COURAGE!
AAAH, THAT WAS SO SCARYYYY.
...
NOSHIRO, PLEASE BE KIND TO OUR NACCHI.
SHE'S A REALLY GREAT GIRL!
BOW
UH, UM.
UH...
SORRY. I...I'VE NEVER HAD A GIRL LIKE ME BEFORE.
SO I DON'T KNOW WHAT TO DO...
WHAT? AAAH, SO CUTE!
BUT, LIKE, I GET THAT!

IT'S OKAY.

YOU CAN GO SLOWLY AND GET TO KNOW EACH OTHER.

Oh! Right! Um...

Please tell me your email!

"WE'LL HAVE SUCH A GOOD TIME!"
HUH?
SO DOES THIS MEAN...
NACCHI
WE'RE GOING OUT...?!
I HAVE A GIRL-FRIEND...?!
TH—

THIS...
...MIGHT NOT HAPPEN AGAIN.
SANADA.
I WONDER IF HE'LL BE MAD ...

THAT'S GOOD THOUGH, RIGHT?
THAT'S GREAT.
...
WHY DID I...
...THINK SANADA WOULD BE MAD?
WHEN MAKOTO TOLD ME HE LIKED ME...
...SO NOW...
...HE THINKS I'M GAY.
UM...
AAAAAAAAH
B—
NOT MY PROB-LEM.
I TOLD YOU NOT TO COME CRYING TO ME, DIDN'T I?
IT'S FINE, THOUGH.
YOU SHOULD TOTALLY GO OUT, YOU KNOW, WITH THE CUTE TENTH GRADER
JOIN THE JUDO TEAM FOR HIM.
OH, RIGHT. THAT...
B—
YOU'RE MAD. SANA-DAAAAA!
I'M TELLING YOU, I DIDN'T SAY ANYTHING ABOUT YOU!
HEY! WAIT UP!
...WAS BECAUSE I ALMOST SAID THAT SANADA'S GAY...
CREPES

THIS TIME, I GUESS ...
...IT'S GOT NOTHING TO DO WITH HIM...
DAI!
...!
HUH?!
IS IT NOT OKAY FOR ME TO CALL YOU THAT?
CALLING YOU "NOSHIRO" ...
IT DOESN'T REALLY FEEL THAT SPECIAL...
"SPECIAL" ...
RIGHT...
SURE, THAT'S OKAY.
REALLY?! HEE HEE HEE...
DAI!

SINCE I STARTED GOING OUT WITH NACCHI...

...MA-KOTO ...
...HAS STOPPED COMING TO SEE ME.

I THINK MORIRIN'S JUST TRYING TO BE CONSIDERATE OF ME.
THAT'S APPAR-ENTLY WHAT'S GOING ON.

I SOME-TIMES SEE HIM WITH THE KIDS FROM HIS CLASS.

HE'S AS POPULAR AS EVER.
HE LOOKS LIKE HE'S HAVING FUN.

2—5
AND SANADA ...

I FEEL LIKE...
...HE'S MORE CHEERFUL NOW.
HE'S ALWAYS TALKING TO THE OTHER PEOPLE IN CLASS.
HE'S ALWAYS LAUGHING.
IT SEEMS IMPOSSI-BLE THAT I HAD TO WORK...
...TO TRY AND MAKE HIM LAUGH.

HUH. YOUR GIRL-FRIEND'S IN BAD-MINTON, NOSHIRO?
ツナマヨ
SO THEN YOU GOTTA WAIT FOR HER UNTIL PRACTICE IS OVER!
HUH?
WELL, I MEAN, YOU GOTTA.
YOU'RE NOT GONNA WALK HOME TOGETHER?
YOU'RE GONNA SEE HER HOME, YEAH?
LUCKY! I'M JEALOUS!

THEN SHE'S TOTALLY GONNA ASK YOU IN...
NGAH. DAMMIT.
CRAP.
DAMN YOU, NOSHI-ROOOOO!

Good luck at practice!
Thanks! Bye!
You wanna try this place?
Sure.

SEE YA, NOSHIRO.

Y—
YEAH ...

SANADA ...
...WALKS HOME WITH YAMA-MOTO A LOT.

I GUESS HE TOLD HER...
...THAT HE'S GAY.

I BET THEY'RE ...
...TOTALLY BONDED NOW.

DAI!
YOU'RE COMING HOME SO LATE THESE DAYS. WHY?!
MOM
OH, JUST ...
I'M WITH A FRIEND ...

SLAM
Aaah
FL
OP
UGH. DAMMIT.
WHOA?! SANADA, YOU'RE SO GOOD!
WE'RE THE PERFECT COMBINATION, HUH!

I'VE GOT SOMEONE "SPECIAL" NOW...
...AND EVERYONE SEEMS HAPPY.
THERE'S NOTHING BAD, BUT...
I MEAN, I SHOULDN'T ...
...BE FEELING SO LONELY.

HEY
?
DAI?
CAN...
CAN WE HOLD HANDS ...?
R-RIGHT.
WE ARE GOING OUT AND ALL...
THAT'S WHAT YOU DO!
....!!
O-OKAY.
EXCUSE ME...

GRAB

AWKWARD

DAI.
YOU'RE KINDA HURTING ME...
!!
!!

S-SORRY!
I'VE NEVER HELD HANDS BEFORE!
PANIC PANIC
NO, IT'S OKAY.
I'M SORRY FOR PUSHING YOU.

BUT...
I WANT THE PERSON I LIKE TO TOUCH ME.
AND I WANT TO TOUCH YOU, SO...

Yaaaaaay!
We did it
...
I UNDER-STAND.

IT'S LIKE...

WHENEVER I TRY TO TOUCH HIM, HE PUSHES ME AWAY.

Ha ha ha!

I GUESS I'M NOT USED TO IT.

SORRY. PRETTY SAD, HUH...

TOUCH HIM?

WHO?

OH...

RIGHT. SANADA.

HE'S IN MY CLASS.

YOU KNOW, THE GUY I'M ALWAYS HANGING OUT WITH...

BUT HE'S...

...JUST A FRIEND, RIGHT?

UH...
Y-YEAH...?
AAAAH! PHEW! THAT SURPRISED ME!
TOUCH THE CREATURES OF THE SEA!
Petting Pool
TAKE A LOOK AT WHAT LIVES IN THE OCEAN!
TAKE A LOOK AT WHAT LIVES IN THE OCEAN!
TAKE A LOOK AT WHAT LIVES IN THE OCEAN!
DON'T DO THAT, DAI.
YOUR FRIENDS AND THE PERSON YOU LIKE ARE DIFFERENT.
YOU DON'T THINK ABOUT YOUR FRIENDS LIKE...
...YOU WANT TO TOUCH THEM OR YOU WANT THEM TO TOUCH YOU, RIGHT?

I THOUGHT YOU LIKED SOMEONE ELSE THERE FOR A MINUTE.
SO YOU DON'T ...
DON'T TOUCH ME.
...WANT TO TOUCH ...
...YOUR FRIENDS ...?
ACTUALLY, WHY WOULD THAT BOTHER YOU, NOSHIRO?

"FRIENDS..."
"...AND THE PERSON YOU LIKE...
...ARE DIFFERENT..."

DO I...
...WANT TO TOUCH SANADA?

I... GUESS SO?
I DON'T KNOW...

WHAT DOES SANADA THINK?
I WISH...
I WISH I COULD TALK TO HIM...

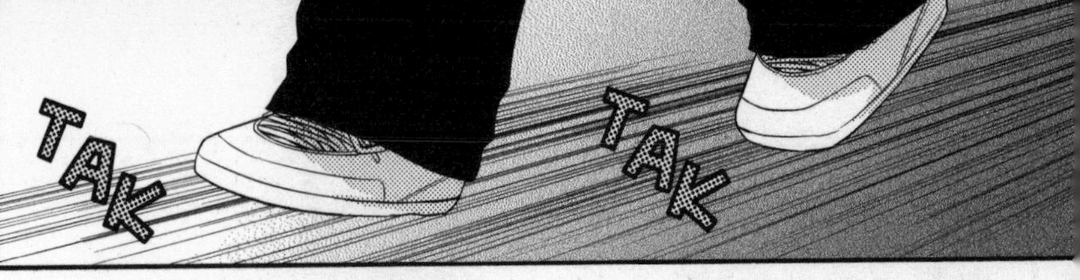


SANADA!

YAMA-MOTO!

HUFF

HUFF

HUFF

NOSHIRO ...!

I'M IN A HURRY. I GOT A THING.
SEE YOU.

KOU.

YOU'VE BEEN IGNORING HIM LATELY.

BUT THAT WAS ALL PRETTY SUDDEN ...
...WITH NOSHIRO, HUH?
I MEAN, A GIRLFRIEND, DATING.
IT DIDN'T SEEM LIKE HE WAS THINKING ABOUT THAT STUFF.

I STILL KINDA CAN'T BELIEVE IT.
NOSHIRO'S ...
...REALLY WITH THAT GIRL...

HE'S GOING OUT WITH A GIRL.
THAT'S "NATURAL."

AAAH.
GIRLS, HUH?
I'VE NEVER GONE OUT WITH A GIRL.

HOW ABOUT WE TRY GOING OUT, TOO?
AYUMI.

WHOMP
OOF

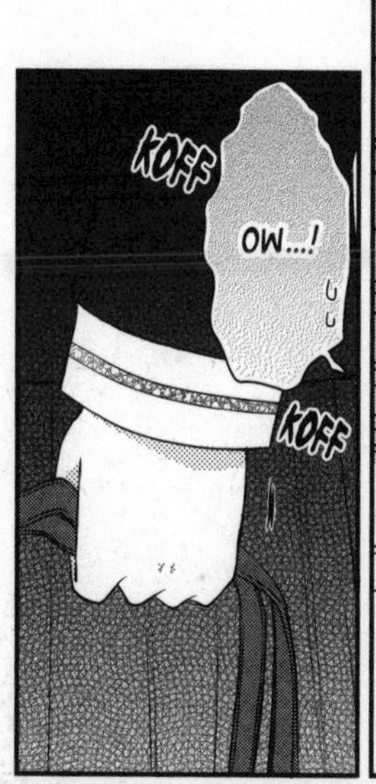
KOFF
OW...!
KOFF

TRY THINKING ABOUT PEOPLE'S FEELINGS!
YOU'RE THE WORST!

DON'T TREAT ME LIKE AN IDIOT!!

THEY'RE IMPORTANT.

OTHER PEOPLE'S FEELINGS.

YOUR FEELINGS!

WHAP
THD

THD
WHAP

HAVEN'T SEEN YOU IN A WHILE, MAKOTO.
RIGHT!
YOU'RE LOOKING GOOD OUT THERE.
RIGHT. I'M REALLY PSYCHED LATELY!

WHY'RE YOU STILL HERE?
Oh...
I'M WAITING FOR NACCHI TO BE DONE WITH PRACTICE.

WE HAVE TO WALK HOME TOGETHER, Y'KNOW?

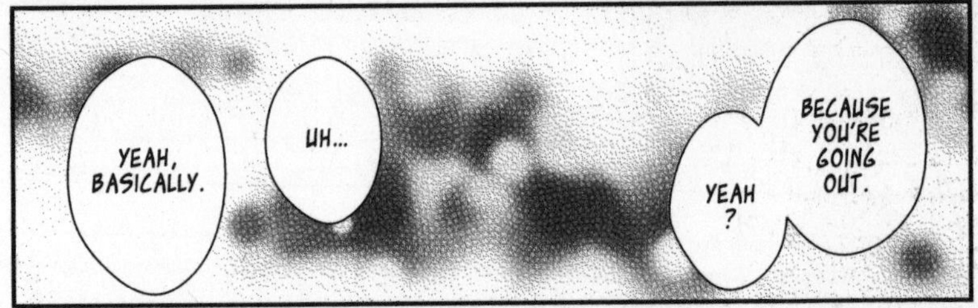
BECAUSE YOU'RE GOING OUT.
YEAH?
UH...
YEAH, BASICALLY.

NOSHIRO.
YOU'RE NOT GOING HOME TOGETHER...

...BECAUSE YOU HAVE TO.
RIGHT?

IT'S 'CAUSE YOU LIKE NACCHI.
AND YOU WANT TO BE WITH HER, RIGHT?
IF IT'S NOT...
...THEN I'M GONNA BE PRETTY MAD AT YOU, Y'KNOW!

THE SKY...
IT'S JUST NOT CLEARING UP, HUH ...

WHAT...
...AM I DOING?

THEY'RE IMPORTANT.

## Final Chapter:
## It's not different. It's the same.

SO LISTEN!
I'VE WANTED TO SEE THIS MOVIE FOR AGES.

BUT IT'S ONLY PLAYING WEEKDAY NIGHTS NOW.
I missed my chance.
MAYBE I CAN JUST SKIP PRACTICE ONE DAY OR SOMETHING.

...DAI, ARE YOU LISTENING?
HUH?!
Y-YEAH. THE MOVIE?
UGH, I'M JUST BLABBING AWAY OVER HERE...
YOU TALK TOO, DAI.
RIGHT.
SORRY...

DING
DING
2—5
KLATTER
See ya!
Have fun at practice!
DING
DING

S—
SANADA ...
YOU'RE NOT HEADING OUT?
...
TODAY ...

I WANTED TO TALK TO YOU.

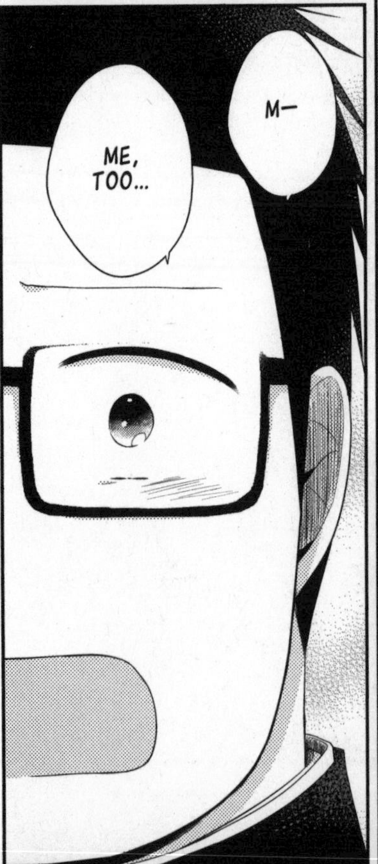

DAI!
BAM
PRACTICE IS CANCELED TODAY!

IF WE HURRY, WE CAN MAKE IT IN TIME FOR THE MOVIE...

OH!

N—
NACCHI...

UM...
TH- THIS IS SANADA.
BOW
H—
HI, I'M AIKAWA.
HEY.

DAI... THE MOVIE ...
OH... Y-YEAH...

GO.
IT...
...DOESN'T HAVE TO BE TODAY OR ANY-THING.

OH...
BUT...

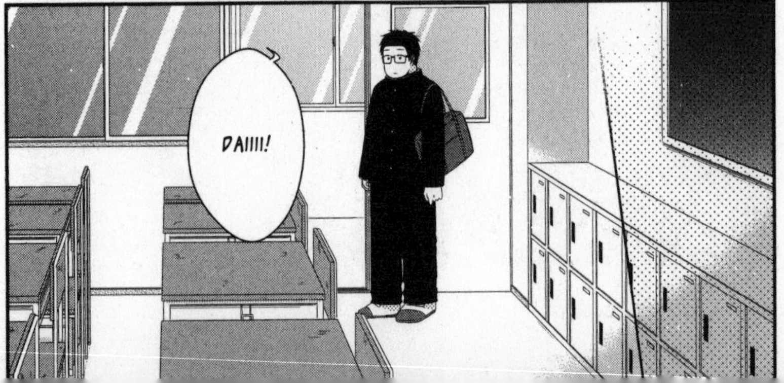
DAIIII!

...
HEY?
WHAT'S SANADA LIKE?
HUH...?

YOU TALKED ABOUT HIM BEFORE, RIGHT?
IF HE'S YOUR FRIEND...
...I JUST FIGURED I SHOULD KNOW HIM, TOO.

WHAT'S HE LIKE...?
SANADA.
HE'S...

HE ALWAYS ...
...LOOKS LIKE HE'S NOT INTERESTED IN OTHER PEOPLE.
AND WHENEVER I ASK HIM SOMETHING ...
...HE ALWAYS DODGES THE QUESTION.
HE ALWAYS ...
...LOOKS LIKE HE'S ANNOYED LISTENING TO ME.
HE'S BASICALLY MAD AT ME ALL THE TIME...

...SAID HE WANTS TO TALK TO ME...

HE'S NEVER SAID ANYTHING LIKE THAT BEFORE!

B-BUT WAIT.
I MEAN, HE SAID IT DIDN'T HAVE TO BE TODAY.
YOU'RE WRONG.
I WANT TO...
...TALK TO HIM RIGHT NOW!
W-WHAT?
YOU AND HIM...
...ARE JUST FRIENDS, RIGHT?
SORRY!
I'M REALLY SORRY!
SORRY!
DASH

...
WHAT IS HE ...
...TO DAI THEN?

SO YOU REALLY DO SIT JUDO OUT, HUH? I'LL SHOW YOU.
LET'S EAT LUNCH TOGETHER!

I WANT TO GET TO KNOW YOU BETTER.

I'LL WAIT UNTIL YOU THINK OF ME AS A FRIEND.

WHY NOT? I'M GLAD I KNOW.

THEN I DON'T GET TO BE WITH YOU, SANADA!

IT'S BECAUSE YOU NEVER TELL ME ANY-THING. I WAS JUST TRYING TO UNDERSTAND!

"IT'D BE GREAT IF WE WERE IN THE SAME CLASS AGAIN, HUH?"

AAAA-AAAAH!!

GOD-DAMMIIIT!!

NOSHIRO!
WHY ARE YOU HERE...?

WHY...?
IT'S JUST, I...

I LIKE YOU, SANADA.
...!
SO...!
WHAT ABOUT IT?!
YOU'RE WRONG!

I LIKE YOU, NOSHIRO.
ME!

I LIKE YOU...
...WAY MORE ...
...THAN YOU LIKE ME!!

IT'S DIFFERENT FROM THE WAY YOU LIKE ME.
IT MAKES ME HAPPY WHEN YOU TOUCH ME.
AND I WAS JEALOUS WHEN I SAW MORINAGA HUGGING YOU.
I WANTED TO KISS YOU.
I'VE WANTED YOU TO BREAK UP WITH YOUR GIRLFRIEND THIS WHOLE TIME!

I WAS WORRIED ...
...YOU'D HATE ME ...
...IF I TOLD YOU.

BECAUSE YOU'RE...
...SPECIAL TO ME!
SANADA.
IT'S NOT DIFFERENT.
IT'S THE SAME.

YOU'RE SPECIAL ...
...TO ME, TOO, SANADA.

AFTER THAT...

...I APOLOGIZED TO NACCHI.
IT'S ONLY NATURAL THAT...
...SHE WAS UPSET, AND HER FRIENDS ...
...WERE MAD AT ME.

AND MAKOTO SAID ...
...HE'D NEVER FORGIVE ME FOR MAKING HIS FRIEND CRY.
BUT HE ALSO SAID...
...HE LIKED IT BETTER WHEN SANADA AND I WERE TOGETHER.
SANADA YELLED AT HIM THAT HE WAS BEING TOO LOUD.

I GUESS SANADA AND YAMAMOTO...
...HAD A LITTLE FIGHT ABOUT SOMETHING.
BUT SANADA...
...APOLOGIZED.
AND THEY MADE UP.
YAMAMOTO SMILED AND SAID...
...THE TWO OF US HAD FINALLY STOPPED BEING STUBBORN.
IT WASN'T UNTIL WAY LATER THAT I REALIZED THIS MUST HAVE BEEN REALLY COMPLICATED...
...BECAUSE OF HOW SHE FELT.
THEN...
...BEFORE I KNEW IT...
...WE WERE IN TWELFTH GRADE.

HUH. SO YOU ENDED UP IN DIFFERENT CLASSES?

THAT'S TOO BAD, HUH?

I'M ACTUALLY WORRIED.

LIKE, MAYBE HE'LL END UP ALONE AGAIN.

ARE YOU MY MOM?

DID YOU MAYBE START DATING?

STRAIGHT.
GAY.

SO...
...ARE WE GOING OUT?
I DON'T KNOW...
...WHAT I AM.

IS THIS "LIKE" AS A FRIEND?
IS IT LOVE?

AND WHAT IS GOING OUT ANYWAY?
I DON'T REALLY GET IT, ACTUALLY.

DUNNO!

I'M HERE.

SANADA'S HERE.

AND IF WE'RE BOTH SPECIAL TO EACH OTHER...

...THEN THAT MAKES ME SUPER HAPPY.

That Sky Blue Feeling / END

This is the final volume! *That Blue Sky Feeling* was created as a snapshot of youth and to show the trials of the heart that come along with being young. I'm truly delighted that this story, which is so important to me, could be told in this form. From the bottom of my heart, a huge thank-you to everyone who supported *Blue Sky*!

Special Thanks

Original story: Okura

Editor

Assistants:
Hina
Takigami

Friends, family, everyone involved with this series

All the readers

Thank you so much!
Coma Hashii

## Dai Noshiro

Born: April 5 (Aries)
5'5", 187 lb., Blood type: O
Grade: Tenth grade
Best subjects: Gym, earth sciences
Worst subject: English
Likes: Having a fun dinner with everyone
Dislikes: Bullies, cowards

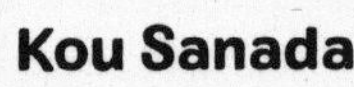

## Kou Sanada

Born: November 7 (Scorpio)
5'5", 127 lb., Blood type: B
Grade: Tenth grade
Best subject: Ethics
Worst subject: Math
Likes: Looking at the view from high places
Dislikes: Standing out, commotions

## Ayumi Yamamoto

Born: August 21 (Leo)
5'1", Blood type: A
Grade: Tenth grade
Best subjects: Japanese history, music
Worst subject: Gym
Likes: Studying at the library
Dislikes: Hearing people badmouth friends

**Komatsu**

Classmate of Noshiro and Sanada. Likes idols.

**Kubota**

Classmate of Noshiro and Sanada. Rich.

**Hidemitsu Chiba**

Born: May 20 (Taurus)
5'9", 240 lb., Blood type: O
Age: 26
Occupation: Office worker
Likes: Cooking, talking to people
Dislikes: Being told what to do and how to do it

**Natsu Aikawa**

Morinaga's classmate. On the badminton team.

**Makoto Morinaga**

Born: March 3 (Pisces)
4'8", 103 lb., Blood type: AB
Grade: Ninth grade
Best subject: Gym
Worst subjects: Everything other than gym
Likes: Judo, reading sports magazines
Dislikes: Studying, tests

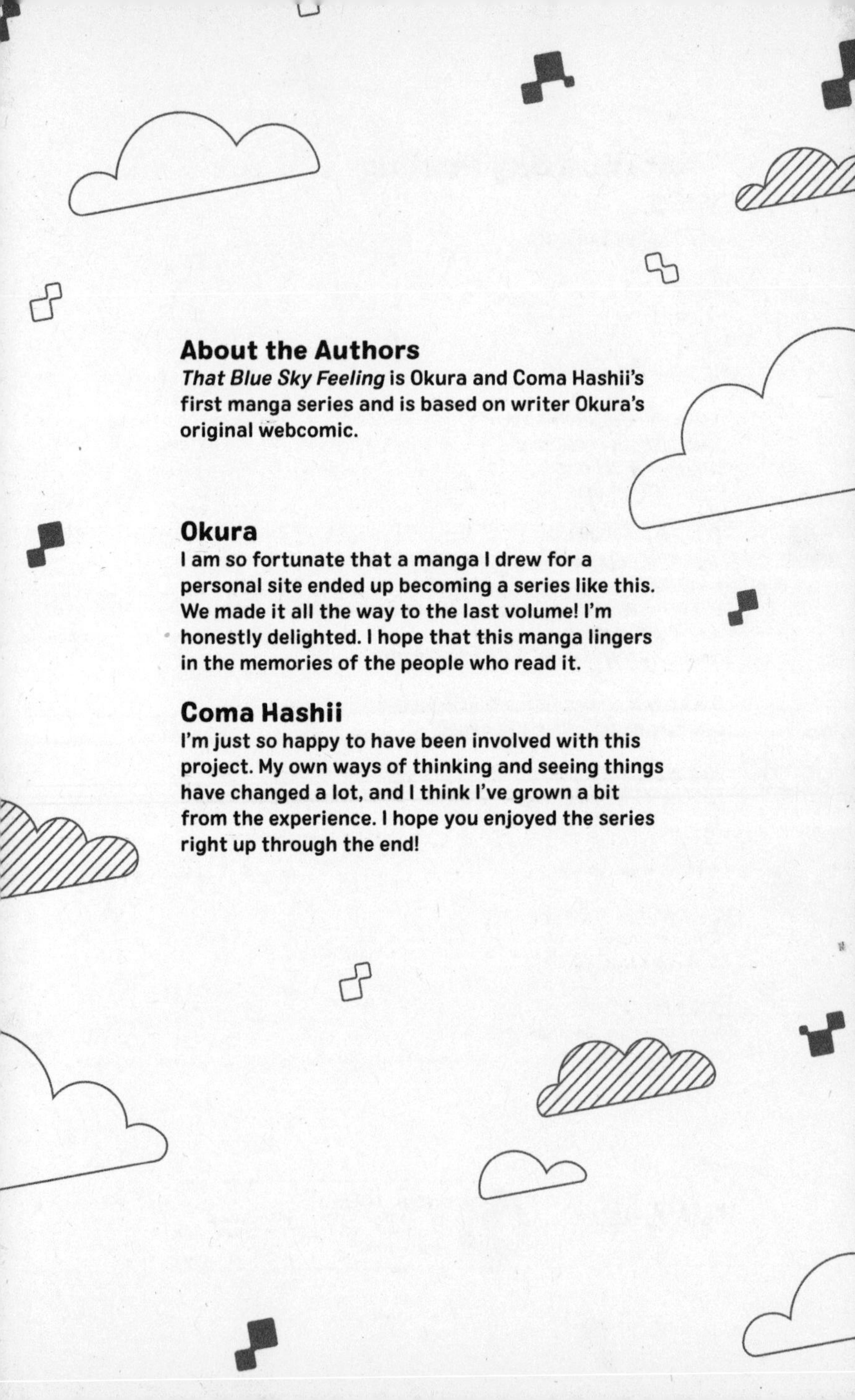

## About the Authors

*That Blue Sky Feeling* is Okura and Coma Hashii's first manga series and is based on writer Okura's original webcomic.

## Okura

I am so fortunate that a manga I drew for a personal site ended up becoming a series like this. We made it all the way to the last volume! I'm honestly delighted. I hope that this manga lingers in the memories of the people who read it.

## Coma Hashii

I'm just so happy to have been involved with this project. My own ways of thinking and seeing things have changed a lot, and I think I've grown a bit from the experience. I hope you enjoyed the series right up through the end!

**Vol. 3**
**VIZ Media Edition**

STORY BY
**Okura**
ART BY
**Coma Hashii**

Translation/Jocelyne Allen
Lettering/Joanna Estep
Design/Yukiko Whitley
Editor/Joel Enos

Printed in the U.S.A.

Published by VIZ Media, LLC
P.O. Box 77010
San Francisco, CA 94107

10 9 8 7 6 5 4 3 2 1
First printing, October 2019

**PARENTAL ADVISORY**
THAT BLUE SKY FEELING is rated T for Teen and is recommended for ages 13 and up. Contains suggestive themes.

Surprise!
You may be reading the wrong way!
It's true: In keeping with the original Japanese comic format, this book reads from right to left—so action, sound effects and word balloons are completely reversed. This preserves the orientation of the original artwork—plus, it's fun! Check out the diagram shown here to get the hang of things, and then turn to the other side of the book to get started!